Healing
Grace

Inspirational Poetry
for Coping & Closure

ISBN 978-1-957087-05-4 (paperback)

Photographs by Michelle G. Stradford

This book is a work of fiction. The names, characters, places, and events are the product of the author's imagination or are used factiously. Any resemblance to actual events, locales, or living or deceased persons is coincidental.

 Published by Sunurchin

Healing Grace

Inspirational Poetry
for Coping & Closure

Michelle G. Stradford

Also, by Michelle G. Stradford:

I'm Rising: Determined. Confident. Powerful.

Rise Unstoppable

Self Love Notes II: Affirming Poetry
& Prose

Self Love Notes: Uplifting Poetry, Affirmations
& Quotes

Waves of You: Love Poems

When Love Rises

DEAR READER

Welcome to *"Healing Grace,"* a collection of poems, affirmations, and meditations that offer comfort and inspiration for your healing journey from heartbreak, adversity, and personal trauma. This book is organized into three chapters, Coping, Restoring, and Closure, providing a gentle guide for those embracing the healing process. My hope is that you will discover yourself in these words and allow your troubles to escape while reading passages silently or speaking affirmations out loud.

The sun dipping beneath the horizon and the endless expanse of the ocean have always filled me with a sense of peace and tranquility. I have included some of my personal photographs to further emphasize the messages of grace and restoration.

Please note that *"Healing Grace"* may contain descriptions that could trigger uncomfortable responses for those who have experienced abuse. Nonetheless, the collection aims to empower readers with the tools needed to navigate their healing journey.

May these pages provide solace and healing for your beautiful soul and inspire you to finally lay claim to the undaunted you.

Sincerely,
Michelle

DEDICATION

*To all who embrace your healing journey
despite the ache, you are deserving of grace.*

Contents

I will never surrender
to life's rage and ire.
My resilience is stoic,
my spirit unshakeable.
Like the hardest diamond,
raw and unpolished,
I remain unbreakable.

Unshakeable

COPING

There are times when the hurting
rushes in too fast
for our shattered hearts to contain.

The heightened level of pain
proves too vast
for our hollowed words to name.

Hollowed

Long after swallowing the biting hurt,
I choke on the aftertaste of regret.
Searing moments come roaring back,
refusing to allow me to forget.

I gulp down glasses of bitter lies,
then pack my gaping wounds
with merciless vows
and fistfuls of defiance.

Denial is key to my survival.

Coping

The best way she knows to heal
is to neutralize the pain,
numb the ability to feel,
and build tall titanium walls
that make her unreachable.

She is locking away her emotions,
and securing the chains to her soul,
so that her winsome heart
will remain unbreachable.

Unbreachable

Instead of resuscitating
my battle-torn heart,
I leave it to fall apart,
hemorrhaging for days
until it lay paralyzed
and lost again in a haze.

Sometimes the bleeding
is all the healing I need.

The Bleeding

She will stop flirting with the flames
that leaves her esteem in ashes.
She is removing all sources of oxygen
feeding the madness
that constantly ignites her pain,
so she will never get burned
with such intensity again.

Flirting with Flames

My wandering wispy girl,
I am on a quest to find you
with wonder still swimming
in your brown eyes.
I escaped youth in fear,
hastily leaving you behind,
before I drowned in tears.

Hold on, younger self;
we are not over yet.
I never intended to abandon you,
nor leave you scared,
while you treaded dark water
alone and gasping for air.

The only way I knew
to make the waves of pain stop
was to block the memory of you
and the daily trauma out.
I sunk fast and lost myself
by submerging our past.
I have resurfaced to retrieve you
so that we can recover at last.

The Rescue

Filling up your thirsty vessel
fizzled my effervescence
and drained me of stored energy.
My positives flowed with ease to you
and left nothing in me but negativity.
After you, there remained no fuel
to run on or space for me to grow.
I have little choice, but to go.

Non-Reciprocal

When your high esteem
and budding love
for yourself ceases growing,
check the source of the seeds
you have been sowing.

The Seeds

I am done stumbling through
the life you coveted, grand illusions
designed by and for you
but never intended to lift me.

I will no longer race breathlessly,
punching punishing hours each day
while struggling to catch up,
trying to do it your way.

All I ever sought or needed
was to believe that the *me*
running this world with you
had already measured up.

This day is the end of me
having to prove repeatedly
that I am invincible,
tough nailed and unbreakable.

Grandly Illuded

If you equate accountability,

transparency and honesty

to being fragile and weak,

you may struggle to forgive,

ever heal or exist in peace.

Finding Peace

Your kisses immersed
my body in pulsing waves,
curling my toes in a vice
until I was lost and dazed.
This. Love. Us. Felt. So. Right.

You circled me in ripples
racing my heartbeats,
marooning me for days,
washing away the trusted vest
I clang to so desperately.

I beseeched the sun's creator
to make it all last.
Then suddenly, our joy
was submerged beneath
your deep and sordid past.

I took a long breath,
held in the lost promises
until your high lies lifted,
then you left me drifting
in a riptide of regrets.
You were an ocean
I never felt coming.

An Ocean

Holding on valiantly
to that never-ending ache
is not remarkably noble.
Self-sacrifice does not always
cause you to grow stronger
or help you attain the goal
you sought the most.

Noble

She resists forcing her mind
to attempt to retrieve
the most painful experiences.
Refusing to remember
is her body's way of healing.

It is her soul's day to believe
that the moment has come
for her to move beyond
that time thieving relic
known as remorse.

Time Thieving Relic

I was dragged unwittingly
along the ragged edge of despair,
but remaining keenly self-aware
of the triggers that cut too deeply
prevented me from bleeding out,
then rapidly spiraling down
a dark victimized hole.

Unwitting

At times your sullen silence

sulks so loudly that you

can no longer hide

your anguish, that raging battle

you keep fighting inside.

So, you work at, meditate on,

then pray for the strength

to expose and heal the hurt.

Sullen Silence

On days like this, you wake up
facing a failure in the mirror,
watching your dreams spiral
down a pipe rushing for the river.
Time races fastest for the reticent.

You have pierced and numbed
your heart so you can no longer
feel the passion for hope linger.
You will not recognize your life
in the face of the lost stranger,
pleading for answers from you.

You close your discontented eyes,
waiting for wisdom to materialize.
Tomorrow you will feel stronger.
But today, you just need the time
to wallow with your pity longer.

Racing Time

Let their evasiveness
be the slap in the face
that jolts your defenses
into a protective position,
seals your resolve into place.

Pay keen attention
to the words they never
even attempt to say.
No response yields a loud
and clear message
intended for you to hear.

Clear Message

If I must strip myself
of substance, shed everything,
shrink to nothing,
watering my self-esteem
down so transparently
that others look through me,
so that you appear stronger,
more capable and wiser,
I'll take a hard pass on you.
I bid you adieu. Goodbye.

Hard Pass

There are days when the struggle
to liberate and forgive myself
threatens to steal my breath.

I blink back the sting in my eyes
feeling angry and hapless,
upon realizing all the layered lies
I tricked myself into believing.

Attempting to protect the ones
I was closest to, enabled the guilty
to smear evil over the souls
of the innocent and defenseless
without earthly consequences.

Protracted Lies

Do not ignore the negative energy
slithering its tendrils into a room.
Escape the impending misery.
Note the glances that avert too soon.

The discomfort you perceive is real.
Your body feels what your eyes
have not been trained to reveal.
Your BS sniffing sensor is wise.

Hear and heed your intuitive guide.

Negative Energy

Yes, I stayed fully knowing
that I should have run.
I thought my love could
erase mistakes, overcome,
and make you treasure
me like no other would.

I believed your sincerity
when you pleaded with me
to release our past
and grant you forgiveness.
I trusted you would never harm me,
diminish my spirit
or bruise my body again.

We made endless attempts
to restart and reshape us
into a fresh new beginning.
I was young, stubborn,
and too naively trusting
to envision a tragic ending.
Not knowing my worth
hurt me tremendously.

My Worth

Prolonging your agony for someone
who does not see or feel you,
nor believe you are worth their trouble,
will never evoke enough joy
to justify your pain and struggle.

Your Agony

The wrath of stinging rain
puttered to a slippery end
as the tumultuous gray clouds
sulked, then rescinded,
ushering the sun in again.
I was blooming, living
and relishing the heat on my skin.

Then the rising silence
began to magnify my pain
until the memory of us
erupted in a roaring flame.
Just when I believed
that I had recovered,
losing you burned me again.

Burning

We shared a connection so bright
that my shadows melted away.
But in time, he dimmed my light
and I could no longer find my way.

Pausing for perspective, I focused my eyes,
and sought guidance from above
to discern what was real or lies.
His tight hold was abusive, not love.

Not Love

Oh, relentless and brutal pain;
what more can you take from me?
You have nearly driven me insane,
hounding me to the edge of infamy.

Why are you attempting
to hijack me, snatch away
my last shred of dignity
Have you no shame?

I carry you in the ache
under my shoulder blades
and feel the menacing weight
of your debilitating hate
rattling my joints when it rains.

I feel you beading up on my skin
at the very mention of him.
I see your bruises in the knocks
that strained the muscles in my back.

You stiffen the clench of my chin
when I fear that I will see him
lurking furtively behind
a remnant of a smile again.

You have usurped my light,
stripped away my energy,
making me feel weak and needy
for what feels like an eternity.

Please stop before you trigger panic.
Your requirements have become
far too demanding.
I long for my brave soul
that you forced me to abandon.

No...you have pushed too far.
The attacks must end.
After all that you have taken,
I will not allow you
to also strip away my sanity.

Too Demanding

My resolve will not be undermined
by your badgering and lies.

No matter how hard you try,
I refuse to give in and will never bow.

Note to self:
End the self-punishment.

Self-Punishment

The weight of carrying
a disturbing truth
can be unbearable.
You sit cowering,
trapped inside
a silent bubble of misery.

Each layer of lie erases
your dignity
causing your integrity to slide
until it fades to near invisible.
You fail to recognize
that you have been gaslit
until it is indefensible.

Gaslit

After spending years of my life
testing claims never proved,
searching for beliefs I could not see,
and avoiding assorted people
who did not suit me,
how is it that I so easily
trusted that you, we
were a sweet alchemy?

My flawed idea of love
blinded my third eye,
causing me to deny
your lies spun into gold
and the bold transgressions
you committed in plain sight.

Transgressions

I rage against the cutting lies
that slashed scars across my heart.
I pretend this smile easily hides
my fear, my shame, and deep hurt
from the battles waged inside.

Coping is an endless struggle
but I am here for the challenge,
as there is no choice but to fight
to win this war to reclaim my life.

Battles Waged

When your voice will not
lay claim to your courage
as the very heart of you
lay bleeding, discouraged,
and your legs refuse
to propel you forward
because your muscles
cannot stop shaking,
hold on with faith.
Your weary soul
will find a way to rise
and deliver the strength
to heal your aching.

Claim Your Courage

While the immediate sting
of their brutal betrayal
had subsided and healed,
harboring resentment
spread like an invasive poison
that nearly destroyed her,
granting the offender
the impact they intended.

Resentment

Despite what you may be going through
there is an abundance of light
still burning brightly inside of you,
You possess gifts the world
has not had the privilege to view.

You have yet to feel the depth of love
so many souls hold for you.
Stay strong; you still belong
amongst this crazy wondrous world.
The universe that craves the taste
of your joyful magic,
exists to drink from your creative soul.

Even when you feel vulnerable,
are running long on empty,
and much in your life goes wrong,
you will always have me to the end.
Release that frustration and anger,
then lean heavily on me for support.

Talk to me, my sister, my brother, friend.
I and countless others see you,
feel your energy and need you.
We will make it work better together.
Heaven can wait a little longer.

I Feel You

When random memories
break down hidden doors
to the long-forgotten rooms
hoarding your collection of regrets,
you may not be on the pathway
to true healing yet.

Hidden Doorways

I conceal the heavy burden
of these stifling secrets
in the marrow of my bones,
while cursing old grievances.

Denial trickles slowly along,
thickening these veins,
risking my well-being,
and shortening my longevity.

I carry this toxic weight
so, the soul-darkening load
will not crush and bury
those whom I so dearly love.

Grievances

Broken relationships,
and untenable homes
can exact more damage
than if you chose
to take the high road
and go at life alone.

The longer you stay,
the more challenging it can become
to unlearn unhealthy patterns
that may lead to dismay
and disrupt your life plan.

When you have done your part,
put in the effort to make it work,
but being with them
continues to hurt,
take the nearest exit.

Nearest Exit

Search behind your mirrored image.

Reach beyond the inhibited illusion

you created for the world's approval

and grab hold of the wild-hearted spirit

you sprang into this world with.

Wild Spirit

Even if they threaten
but never hit you,
anyone who attempts
to control your every move
is a dangerous person.
Abusers leave no room
for you to breathe.

Dictating your mood,
what you should think,
the food to consume,
or how much you drink
is manipulative
and emotionally cruel.

You were born to live
and roam the earth freely,
not to be held captive
as someone's possession.
Get out now
before their obsession
renders you
completely defenseless.

No Room

We swallow our aches in silence,

choking them down

like a bitter poison

to numb our surly emotions.

Bitter Poison

You are allowed to desist
investing in relationships
where the other person resists,
rarely initiates contact,
and dismisses your bond's existence.

They only seek connection
to obtain favors and gifts,
or to be rescued from rejection,
yet are unavailable to support you
if your esteem needs protecting.

Call it what it is named;
harmful unbalanced benefits
and a one-sided arrangement,
in which you are no longer
willing to feel estranged.

Estranged

I hoard agitated emotions,

hiding and stacking them between

dusty pages of foregone notions,

worn pretenses and torn promises.

I bind each hurtful grievance

into the thick of my layers of skin,

forming leathered boundaries

that envelops me in full protection.

Torn Pretenses

It is perplexing that a photograph
can imprison you in the past
stirring up an emotional tornado
that sucks you into its vortex,
leaving you bewildered
and spinning
amongst breath-sucking
conflicts
you barely noticed existed.

Knowing your defensive triggers
will aid you in navigating
farther away
from a tumultuous
filled day
to avoid the nostalgic
tripping.

Triggers

Though we desperately need
those whom we love completely
to understand that our souls hold
palpable and insufferable pain,
we know they cannot sit in it with us,
nor feel the fire burning
beneath our skin.

Fire Beneath

Healing Grace

Like a vintage letter,
I crumple, then curl inwardly,
carefully closing me tight.
I wrap my worries
in prayers and song sheets
loosely bound
in the pages of a hymnal.

I pray for protection
of my spiritual essence,
as it is all that I recovered
after my earthborn innocence
went missing without witness,
while the holy slept
under the cover of silence.

No Witnesses

Being dragged up a flight of stairs
was a terrifying experience.
How did I descend so low,
bend to being violently lifted
over life's splintering rungs
by the root of my hair?

I tripped over dangerous treads
to the bottom of despair.
A freshly sprang woman,
carefree and optimistic,
I believed I had found my prince,
until my happy upended.

I was too young to know that real love
rarely descended to unhinged and cruel.
I should have reserved the energy
that still provided me with fuel
and used it to save me
instead of willing him to change.

I was tormentingly slow to realize
life with him would never get better
and that my forever after
was an impending disaster.
Even when the bruises healed,
I could not end the bleeding,
would not stop believing
that my love was strong enough
to save me and fill the voids in him.

Abusers of trust thrive on power.
Complete control only gets them higher.
Too stunned to cry for help,
I suffered in dismayed silence.
Even when friends and coworkers
noticed telling differences,
the way my smile twisted into a wince,
I assured them I was okay.
Professed I had carelessly slipped,
slammed my wrist into a door,
or tripped and fell to the floor.

When my body became too thin,
I lied that my frail weight
had been purposeful.
I inhaled his gaslighting,
transforming into
a highly functioning denier.
Ashamed I had chosen the wrong one,
I blamed myself and wallowed
in a stupor of stunned disbelief.

My body and mind understood
it was way past time to run,
that I needed to abruptly end it,
but my heart had not known
how to process the concept
of new love tainting
then becoming dangerous.
Then finally, the survivor
in me shifted...
My veil of denial lifted.

Veil of Denial

Why does my mind place such reliance

in my petulant and distant past

when I ceased looking for guidance

from yesterday's wayward paths?

Wayward

These cascades of tears
are not shed in vain,
they are the first stage
of my pierced heart in healing.

When acknowledging
freshly unleashed pain,
my ragged breaths reach
to find how deep the stab runs.

Processing Pain

That which you believe
you cannot be whole without
might be the very start
of breaking yourself apart.

Wholeness

Too often, you recognize
the blazing red flags
only to ignore them,
putting your physical
and emotional safety in peril.

Self-love is making
your wellbeing paramount
by placing your safety
above granting someone
the benefit of the doubt.

If the situation raises alarms,
does not look or feel right
create a plan today,
and swiftly remove
yourself from harm's way.

Blazing Red Flags

I am searching for an out,
release from the twisted past,
an escape route to a future
that sets me on an open path
long enough to outrun
my abuser's twisted grasp,
so I can finally unleash
my unchained wrath.

Unchained Wrath

When it is too difficult
to admit or impart
your life-sustaining needs
without falling apart,
it is absolutely okay
to steel yourself in silence
as your chosen way
of processing and coping.

Once you are strong enough
to manage the pain,
you can peel open
your old bandages
to allow someone you trust
help assess the damage.

Assess the Damage

It is the betrayal of trust
and the stripping away
of my innate innocence
that has lifted my suspicions
of the intentions of many adults.

In the formative years
following my birth,
instead of the needed nurture
men often proved
to be covert perverts.

After years of coping
and esteem mending,
my self-healing mantra
now breathes fire into me.

Keep your warped
form of inhuman touch
and your body parts
to yourself.

You are the tragedy
from whom I needed
the most protection.

Betrayal of Trust

Continually lessening your needs

to co-exist with someone peacefully

is a precarious fluidity

that eventually becomes unlivable.

Unlivable

You spend years defining who you are,
what is most important to you,
and establishing where you are going.

You finally meet someone promising,
but they become menacing,
treating you with disrespect and derision.

They cause you to question yourself,
blaming you for the hurt, you're feeling,
then attempt to convince you
that you are an unworthy being.

Never retain anyone in your life
who initially makes you feel
you are experiencing heaven,
then tramples you into the earth.

You are deserving of reciprocal love,
the kind that's rare and unconditional.
Putting your well-being first
is a trust that is non-negotiable.

Non-Negotiable

I am painstakingly
making my way through
the emotional ruins
of a life of resistance,
climbing over broken
pieces of myself
to reassemble
a more durable existence.

Broken Pieces

Your backhanded compliments
cracked in my ear like a club.
I do not know where you learned
that offensive behavior,
but this is decidedly not love.

It hurts that you consistently
and purposely strike out at me
when *you* feel low or unworthy.

I refuse to be berated again
and have had enough of nonsense.
I am bringing us to an end.

Enough

When your eyes begin to sting
and that unnamed something
inside of you suddenly breaks
allowing raw emotions to rush through
your locked floodgates,
know that a deep cleansing
was overdue to help replenish you.
Refuse to hold back anything.
Allow your tears to wash you anew.

Deep Cleansing

RESTORING

Each desperate hour
stumbles over the next
while time collapses.
I gasp for another breath,
lungs drunk from racing,
competing with myself.

Wrestling, then chasing,
I am defeating these demons
at their rigged life test
before my sun is ready to set.
My heart will beat life into me
until not one dream is left.

Time Collapses

There are few things as bitter

as the taste of regret

burning this hole in my chest.

Raw emotions churn

to ensure I finally learn

to get my priorities in check.

Taste of Regret

Even if you were born
with the tiniest of wings,

you were never meant to conform

or be grounded in a nest.

Resist remaining confined

by the gravity of your tests.

Gravity

Healing Grace

The wounds endured without remedy
deepened and multiplied,
allowing pain to empty
into the reservoir
that supplied my thirsty soul.

Pretending that I was fine
tainted my life source,
nearly draining me dry.
With care, over time,
I will heal and be restored.

Remedy

If ever you feel constricted,

use the talents you were gifted.

Flex and extend your full span.

Your untethered spirit

will airlift you to wherever

in life, you are destined.

Full Span

When it is far too dark

for you to find the light

still burning low in your heart,

it may be time to part

with the gas lights

that have been

eclipsing your spirit.

Time to Part

They marvel at her allure,
cool demeanor and poised beauty.
Her weighted words
can level great wrongs,
her stare silences tongues
without debate or discussion.

But beneath her ice-slicked mountain
lay an ominous simmer.
Resolve is melting, anger's rising,
her earned grace holds back pressure,
the threat of a fiery eruption.
She is a volcano, readied for destruction.

Simmering

It is in the delicious silence
after all my head chatter quiets
that I discover hidden morsels
of wisdom sagely stirring
in my cup of solitude.
The taste of my spirited essence
is the sweetest solace.

Sweet Solace

Refuse to listen
to the misogynist lyrics,
trumped-up stories
and altered images that are illicit
infusing the air you breathe
with the repeated rejection,
the biting whispers
in hushed undertones
and unfiltered reflections
that leave a girl's esteem
in a twisted wreckage.

Shut out the endless sermons
that bore into your brain
like a tiresome earworm.
Ignore the preaching
that original sin was born
from her bite of the apple
to all relationships gone wrong,
blaming the ills of the world
on the very existence
of every strong-willed woman.

Some men cannot handle
the power you wield
simply having been born
capable of growing, nurturing
and delivering a human.

They will continue to charge
at you and come for you
because their ultimate goal
is to hold you back, penned down,
hemmed in beneath them.
Forget all of that.
You are the reckoning.
Rise up and fight like one.

Reckoning

My fire runs so hot and wild,
They will never contain me.
I am burning down anything
that tries to harm me indiscriminately.

To survival, I am no stranger.
This frenzied rage refuses to die
until the last patch of danger
is scorched and burned putrid dry.

My Wildfire

Sometimes the wounds
of trauma never entirely mend.
Keep your defenses ready;
there will be more battles to win.
You must keep saving yourself
until your last sunrise ends.

Sunrise Ends

It can be tough to will your way
out of life's oppressions,
or send shame packing
following a tearful confession.

Summon the strength
to fight your way back
and reinforce your defenses
against self-inflicted attacks.

Only you hold the power
to attain your breakthrough
by banishing harmful habits
that constantly afflict you.

Breakthrough

The moment when you fully
appreciate that being an expert
at pretense, is at once
your liberating salvation
and cowering
defense mechanism,
is the start of healing.

Pretense

Your ability to push through it,
pretend abuse doesn't still hurt,
fake success until you get it,
grin graciously despite the hits,
all leave deep scars on your psyche.
Despite your steel and strength
You won't find peace that is authentic
without losing those who are demented.

Authentic Peace

Self-sacrifice
can carry a high price
that undermines honor
if you destroy yourself
in the process.

Price of Sacrifice

A layer beneath your mistakes
is where you will uncover
life's most profound meaning.
Peel back that thin skin
and sink into your discomfort.

Feel those poor decisions
submerge you deeper,
threatening to fill your lungs,
as they drown you in dread.
You chose a poor path for a reason.
Lie in the stink you created
to retrieve your life lesson.

Sit still until the air stifles,
and you grow uncomfortable.
Stand in the mess you made
just long enough
that your lower back stiffens,
and those leg muscles grow rigid.

Examine the wrong
from multiple perspectives
to determine why it lacked wisdom.
Then trust that you have grown enough
to never repeat your past.
Self-examining brings forth
cathartic transformations.
Be proud of yourself.

Cathartic

Stop showing up when neither
your absence or presence
matter at all to them.

Their ambivalence holds
crucial lessons.
Filtering out what you prefer
not to see or hear
can be detrimental.

Listen intentionally
and respond definitively.

Ambivalent

She gazed in the mirror
assessing her figure,
blinking back the tears,
remembering how the words cut
when he cruelly stoked her fears.

He proclaimed she would
never be enough,
because her looks and curves
would not measure up
to the women he preferred.

It took some work to get there,
to learn to appreciate
that her ample shape
embodied an alluring woman
built of unwavering strength.

Beauty Embodied

Losing me became my foulest fear.
I slipped through the dark folds,
no longer able to believe
my strength would hold.

Lost was the faith that healing prayers
or hope could sustain me.
Friends and family who had always
centered me, faded to invisible.

Shock rendered my soul black.
I could not determine how
to summon my fire back.
Somehow, there remained a flicker.

The Folds

You slide into that feeling,
an irritating uneasy
weaves its way back again,
tugging and teasing
at your tattered edges.

Stress slows your pace
as you filter your thoughts
like grains of beach sand
sliding through your hands.

You attempt but fail to catch
the magical moments
of your hurried existence
as they fall like grains to the bottom
of a vintage hourglass.

When the weight of the day
lands too heavy upon you,
nestle into your favorite chair
in your version of wilderness.

Settle in for some healing
amid pure air and a shower
of natural cleansing.
Relax as the clarifying water
seeps peace into your skin.

No need to dry your eyes,
wipe away life's stains,
or feign being inspired.
Sit and revel in just being
and breathing in this moment.
You have earned your escape.

Escapism

I am more than capable
of repairing the breaks
threatening to end me.
I will learn from past mistakes
and rely on faith to help me see.
The old, flawed path I will forsake
and set a new course
for a more significant life stake.

I will play music in the dark
without losing myself there.
I will surrender to my heart
and sing offkey without a care.
I am ready for the challenge,
to escape these shadows,
rebuild my shattered life
and find my way again.
I am here for the win.

For the Win

After misplacing multiple years
trying to hold back the hurt,
my wall of courage gave way
to a torrent of salty tears,
cleansing dark memories away.

My timely breakthrough
ushered in a new wave,
a novel approach to coping.
I am beginning my regrowth
by recapturing once lost hope.

Regrowth

A deep dive below my surface
uncovered imperfections
and hidden dangers
that I may be ill-prepared
to face and accept.

Submerging myself
into my sea of confusion
will require deep breathing,
and an indomitable heart
strong enough to purge
and capsize anything
that should never rise
to the surface again.

Below the Surface

I pray for this storm to end.
But if logic fails me
and the hurt keeps pouring,
I will stop treading water,
then take a deeper dive
beneath my wounds.

I will draw in a long breath,
then swim with the current
to avoid drowning
inside my pain.
Strength, please continue
to carry me by faith.
Amen.

Strength Prayer

Surrender your troubles to the storm.
Let the deluge rinse away the pain
wash you with reassuring calm,
urging you to shed all shame.
The fresh cleansing waters will comfort
and shower you with promise again.

Slowly spill each burden, releasing them
into the earth's thirsty core.
Allow your mind to follow and flow
to where the river knows
how to efficiently filter,
leach out and wash your worries.

When your sorrows, at last, lay to rest
deep beneath beds of sediment,
fleeting peace will finally settle
into the smoothness of your bones.
This is how the most resilient souls
are restored or newly formed.

Sediments

I am a new blend of seasons
knee-deep in confusion,
bridging the divide between
my stunted Winter of freezing
and the promise of Spring,
chirping with the sounds
of new life beginning.

My frayed emotions converge
on a Summer of searching,
sending me back to places
I have previously seen,
experiences that I tried to exist in,
yet never could feel anything.

I am on a journey, a mission
to restore me to full bloom
before the rustling Fall descends.

New Season

The remedy is going to hurt.

But if you act with humility,

you will push through the work

and reclaim your dignity.

Though you may wish to turn back,

your renewal will be worth

the effort to remain on track.

Renewal

As long as your crimson blood
is coursing through strong veins
steadily pulsing and warm,
you will never become
too injured or far gone
to recapture the wonder
of your spirited soul.

Though you may be battling
a heart-stopping illness
or barely clinging to a miracle,
fight every second to survive.
You give special meaning
and purpose to someone's life.
Loving hard is a long game.

Long Game

You wore your Summer smile
sunny bright, and wide,
heating up the chilly evening,
amber burning in your brown eyes.
We whispered secrets beneath
the yellow buzz of streetlamps.

I bloomed into a peach peony
while basking in your glow,
unfurling my soft petals
as I pulled you in close.

I could not have then imagined
that your light would soon dim,
to a dark and faded Fall frown,
leaving my declarations of love
fluttering in the November wind.

You abandoned my heart,
and left me for frozen
beneath your Winter snow.
I trust in the healing of Spring,
the magic of reawakening and know
I will rebound and touch the sky
in unbridled new growth.

Rebound

I bind soothing words
of affirmations and comfort
around my aching soul
after opening one more
promising door,
only to watch lasting love
escape my grasp once more.

I will capture the next heart
where the fireflies glow,
then hold it in a glass jar
until my soul alights
and is completely restored.

Glass Jar

She crawled nonstop in the dark,
until light sifted through the leaves
finally emerging on the other side,
grateful for what she had achieved.

Her journey was not an easy one.
The price she paid was steep.
The prize of preserving her sanity
was a life of hard-fought freedom.

Her self-love was a beacon
as she shined aglow with pride,
a reminder that with untiring courage,
she may falter and fall, but never fail.

Beacon of Love

Please do not collapse inwardly
or extinguish your fire
out of fear of living
and slowly wither
down to a remnant
of the flame you once were.

Re-ignite. Re-claim.
Do not allow a cowardly abuser
to force you to become
their repeat victim
by giving up your spirit.
Never quit on you.

Never Quit

Obsessive focus on what happened to me
was seizing all my energy.
Searching out a motive for their cruelty
continued to reopen sealed wounds,
and restarted the bleeding.

Infuriated that there would never
be atonement for my offenders,
I struggled to understand my role
and ownership in my repeated undoing.

Intense self-observing, controlled breathing,
and meditation allowed me to focus
and finally, see the obstacles
encumbering and injuring me.

My vision sharpened to look beyond
the healing journey before me
and visualize a fantastic future
my perpetual victim mindset
had not allowed me to see.

Sharpened Vision

Summon your fortitude
to move forward,
even when disheartened
that your most fragile parts
keep breaking open.

Heal the wound swiftly
so it does not kill off
your fighting spirit.
Then keep moving.
Never remain still.

Fighting Spirit

After having been stripped
of all I have known,
I am left lost and alone,
without my people
and what I knew as home.
I ride the wayward wind
searching for a reason
to ever soar again,
or to love me in the end.

I consider the truism
that joy germinates
from the simple moments
and is never sustained
in grandstanding flashes.
Bliss must smolder in my bones
before it can ignite and radiate,
then light fire to my soul.

I sense my energy shifting,
as these burdens lighten.
I am feeling uplifted,
and incredibly grateful
for this new chance at living
that I have been gifted.

Joy Germinates

In the morrow, when I awake
I shall fully re-open
then throw wide my gates
at the top of the sunlit hour.

I will close my eyes and recapture
unimaginable childlike joy
after decades of being trapped
between the hours before dawn.

I will turn towards the sky
like an eager sunflower,
happily basking in the high
from the glow of my recovered smile.

Eager Sunflower

Though her skin carries the scars of a life
she no longer recognized as her own,
she willed herself to leave it all behind,
start the arduous journey to thriving alone.

She sprinted with unwavering focus and grit,
shedding the weight of years of mistreatment.
Leaping past hurdles, she defied all limits
and sped forward to a life of boundless freedom.

Forward to Freedom

Protect what ignites your heart
so you can turn up your light
holding it high above the dark
to locate threats in the night.

Stand ready to pierce the injustices
that cause you disdain
and incite your anguish.
Then set a torch to their madness.

Do everything you can manage
to avoid being engulfed whole
when a blanket of sadness
threatens to suffocate your soul.

Your Torch

Though you have been denied
life's simplest of joys
and abandoned yourself
as a hopeless cause,
it is past time for a reset.

It may be difficult for you
to escape the claws of the past,
but call on your courage
to take a faithful step forward.
Treating your mind and body
with pampering and kindness
will put you on the path
to uncover the strength
you inherently possess.

Choosing a favorite form
of self-care therapy
is treating yourself with love
and deserved dignity.

Simple Joys

Please dry that lone tear
before a flash flood begins.
Shrug away your rising fear
to prevent dread from setting in.

Fixing the mess, you made
commands immediate action.
Confusion will begin to fade
as your valor gains traction.

From this moment forward
you will be standing firm for you,
breaking depression's cycle
by seeing each problem through.

Commanded Action

She is prioritizing her safety
by not wasting a second of time
wondering if the danger is real
or whether she's lost her mind.

She is finally protecting herself
from all toxic relationships,
by placing her mental health
and physical wellness first.

She refuses to allow herself
to be used and manipulated,
consistently put down,
jerked around or baited.

She is learning to safeguard
her well-being with hard boundaries
to accelerate her healing.
She is turning her life around.

Safeguarding

Somedays, despite
how bright your shine,
the waning gilded sun
just continues to slip beyond
your desperate grasp,
sliding off the horizon
as it sinks into the blue shadows
of a faded depression.

Place your faith in a promise
that hope in tomorrow
will lift away today's sorrow.
Fight off the despair
by filling evenings with prayer.
You will awake to a sunrise
ushering in that blinding future
you were building all along.

Blinding Future

After intense internal debate
and months of mental wrangling,
I have grown...gotten over it.
Yes, despite the lingering ache,
the sorrow I yet harbor
for a relationship that was ill-fated.
My near-perfect human
will never feel me again,
or see me in his
deepest reflections.

He will not sense my heart rising
with his in excited unison
as we stage an escape
from our earthly troubles.
He won't experience floating carefree
above the azure horizon
on our secret rendezvous
in a red-hot air balloon.
Maybe, I still have a way to travel
on my heartbreak journey.

Helium Journey

Cease cowering in the background.
Confront your frightening truth.
A new and more potent version of you
will re-emerge to plow through
whatever it is that is blocking you.

Confrontation

When agony pierces so deeply
that it throbs in cadence
beneath your skin and teeth,
making existing feel untenable
and robbing you of joy,
please tell me.

Friend, I stand here for you.
Suffering in silence only raises
the volume of your pain,
amplifying shame
and drowning out logic.

You must not always be strong.
Leaning on others for support
is one of the most courageous
and selfless acts you can perform.

Please allow me the honor
of being the rock that anchors you
stacking favor in your corner.

Anchors

Healing Grace

There comes a time in your life
when you must stifle the tears,
smother the agony and set hurt aside
for days, months, and often years
to keep moving and breathing.

In the fight to survive,
please try to outlast your fear.
Continue to hold on tight.

There will be ample time
for self-compassion
and a cleansing cry
after you make it safely
to the other side.

Hold On

Ambushed by life changes,
my energy is zapped.
I am frozen, emotionless
wrung out, feeling hapless.

These murky days
have left me dampened
in a dizzying daze,
a flimsy weakling
fleeing the ravages of change.

Though unwelcomed,
this disruption proved liberating.
I learned to shift my perspective,
a sharpened eye view
to see that my gray skies
would not remain stormy.

The sun returned in full rotation.
The dawn of infinite possibilities
ignited a rousing spirit
that moved and renewed me.

Dawning Possibilities

When you forgive yourself,
all that sadness and anger,
those dark clouds that linger,
simply disperse and scatter.

Focus your frustrated energy
on breaking apart the chains,
whether generational injury
or self-inflicted disdain.

Let your healing release you
and ease some of the pain,
allow you to process the truth
so you can move freely again.

Forgive You

When your heart breaks apart
you find anything that numbs
to soften the shakes, erase the loss.
You lead yourself to the edge
of the night searching for whys,
doubting every judgment,
questioning your looks and appeal.

You watch your once high esteem
drop far too low to sustain
a relationship for any season.
You close yourself off and commit
to exist without companionship,
embracing a life of chastity.

Though you feel like crap,
you know you must move dutifully
through the pain and find a reason
to regain your perspective.
You fight to achieve stability,
balance and any semblance of peace.

You remember that your heart
cannot beat its strongest
if you overprotect it.
So, you get on with the healing,
anticipating the feel of love coursing
freely through your veins again.

Overprotect

The way you embrace today,
cope with life's challenges
by the action you take
will paint the captivating portrait
of whom you are destined
to become tomorrow.

What do you want to be
on the other side
of pain and struggle?
Broken and wrought
with bitterness
or stoic and charging ahead
in blinding faith?

Which face will you see?
What version of you will you be?

Which Face

Remain present for you today.
Permit yourself to stroll along a brook.
Pause your busyness to frolic in the rain.

Read that indulgent fantasy book.
Avoid analyzing your pain
until you are emboldened and ready.

Listen to your favorite music.
Dance and turn until you are dizzy.
Resist cluttering your thoughts
with to-do lists and past regrets.

Though you cannot reverse time,
slowing down both your body
and your overactive mind
is vital to reaching full healing.

Full Healing

I put in the required work
each day that I am gifted
to reclaim my worth,
and raise up my spirits.

I rise with a glint of the sun
shining in my eyes,
joy jumping off my tongue
and promptly help myself
to a giant serving
of positive assertions.

Choking back fears, I swallow
a glass of fresh-squeezed dignity.
Then dismantle one burden
before it can destroy me.
Restoring myself is a process.

Dismantle Burdens

Before I could fully heal,
I slowly descended
deep into a heap of brokenness,
where this fresh pain could be tended
and weathered.
I lay dormant while my heart recovered
until it relearned how to feel,
then again wandered carefree,
and unprotected.

Brokenness

When your world moves too rapidly
unraveling in spirals,
leaving you breathless,
unable to catch hold
of a coherent thought,
close your eyes, take a rest
to end the spinning.

Invoke a serene vision
of your mind flowing at ease
alongside a blue rippling lake
and her swaying trees.

Picture your stress-filled moments
as an enormous blank canvas
and paint the colors of peace
in the green and yellow splatters
that your intuition sees.

Dismiss unsettling thoughts
by ordering them away.
Take your breath back,
and slowly exhale the fear.
Revel in the perfect still.

Exhale Fear

I am high-stepping it away
from that eight to five
out of the aim of rapid-fire days
and their merciless grind
to add more life to my years,
harvest my precious time,
and water my soul in happy tears.

It is past time for me to shine
so I shall soon vacate.
Yes, I'll replenish my mind
with some healing cleansing.

High Stepping

Your fantastical brain
can magically bury things
that are too painful
to process or understand.

Oblivion is your protective shield
to keep you from tripping over bombs
as you navigate through life.

Uncovering forgotten trauma today
is unlikely to make it less hazardous
than it was in your lost days.

Your mental strength and maturity
will guide you safely through
your emotional mind fields.

Trust your seasoned perspective
and the ability to detect
and diffuse emotional explosives.

Oblivion

Igniting a flame in you today
is more paramount
and precious than anything.
Hold steady to your core
in this pivotal moment.

Truly experience yourself
in this now,
this rare hour,
like there are no promises
left for tomorrow.

Your revealing light will eclipse
all future sorrows.

No Promises

Sometimes courage appears
futile and feels clueless.
You keep driving forward,
nonetheless.

Though you may feel off track,
remaining stuck in neutral
and merely revving your pedal
is sure to roll you back.
Just press on.

Press On

Michelle G. Stradford

CLOSURE

The lioness roar in you
is neither missing nor broken,
she crouches beneath your skin,
serene and semi-frozen
waiting to be summoned again
by your wise whisper
at the precise time required.

The power held in your silence
is exacting and insistent.
Just listen intently.

Wise Whispers

I deserve and need to be loved
in a way that you never would.

The thinner I stretched myself for you,
the less of me I could feel.

Burying my hopes inside of you
is no longer how I choose to live.

I Choose

Oh, battered heart of mine,
warden of youthful confidences,
protector of my low moments,
relieve me of this confusion.

Someday my sweet truth
will flow like blended red wine
pouring out justice in unison,
summarily numbing time,
while uncorking stifled minds.

Barrels of fermented feelings
will bleed freely,
as I watch my reserves
poison the guilty
and preserve the innocent.

Bleed Freely

Though the depth of my burdens

will remain unspoken,

I am the epitome of strength.

Repeatedly battered and bent,

I stand tall, still unbroken.

Still Unbroken

Yes, this world tried to break you in two.
Entering a promising relationship
should have given comfort to you.
Yet, you found yourself vulnerable,
lost, and feeling defenseless.

You were injured and felt used.
Living, yet barely existing,
was a difficult and painful truth.

You gathered up your shattered esteem,
moved swiftly and broke free.
Escaping the cruelty was far from easy,
yet you made it through.
Celebrate reclaiming you.

Reclaiming You

I shall never mind the struggle
as I labor to climb even higher,
for I am worth the trouble.
Besides, the view
from here is inspiring.

Worth the Trouble

Messy, maddening, and meaningful.
Vessels hanging lose,
beats skipping a sad melody.
Mending my battered heart
might be improbable
and may prove impossible,
but I am screaming with jubilance
that I have experienced
soul connecting love,
life-affirming lust,
painfilled deep loss,
and lasting lessons,
permitting me the reward
of living fearlessly.
Loving wild and free
has yet to kill me.

Life Affirming

Long-endured pain

can shatter souls.

Doing the difficult work

to finally mend

will keep you whole.

Shatter Souls

Loving without conditions
has never meant
I am willing
to be used up and abused
or that a relationship
with me
does not require
your inherent trust.

While there is no need
for a binding contract,
we must be clear
on love's definition
before moving forward.
Let us both check
our baggage
for this trip
and trust our connection
will be lasting.

Definitions

The most profound soul cleansing,
and growth transforming
moment for her
was no longer fearing
that feeling emotionally needy
was her weakness.

Sustained love and support
is a core need for every human.
Should she find herself deficient,
she will fill up on love internally.

Emotional Needs

No matter how fast I run,
nor how far I roam,
these knowing bones
will never forget the hell
from whence I have come.

Traces of who I once was
and all that I have survived
still surge through me
in swells of pride.
Restless grit races in my blood.

I am humbly grateful
to have forged
my lived experience
into a woman of endurance.

Woman of Endurance

Becoming a valiant warrior
was not a conscious choice
that was mine to make.
I instinctively fought viciously
to survive sustained attacks.
My strength is innate.

Valiant

She delights in the steps
that move her feet forward,
is frustrated by the remorse
still holding her hostage.

She sings her graces
for the lithe and sturdy legs
she has been granted
to dance through life undaunted.

Despite disappointments and wrongs,
she is grateful and uplifted
by every new day to heal
and live the life she is gifted.

Dance of Life

The newly formed hardened skin
from all that bruising and blistering,
has built you into a tough
and a far sturdier version
of an already fierce contender.

Never accept your burdens
as an obstacle to overcome,
but as a growth portal
to prepare you for your future.

Growth Portal

Your mistakes and struggles
are as much a part of you
as your victories and glory.

Those holes riddling your heart
will resist healing until you fill
in the remainder of your story.

We are all a collection
of sad and joyful moments.
You own your manuscript.

Write, then fully inhabit
the life you have imagined.

Your Manuscript

I kiss old mistakes goodbye.
They no longer hold the power
to frighten me with their ire,
and neither choke,
harm or burn me
like an untended fire.

Phantom failures will no longer
startle me awake
from a sweaty slumber
inside a nightmare of regret.
No, my future is secured.
I finally neutralized the threat.

Neutralized

It is a gut-wrenching
journey to recover
from disloyal betrayal
or outright cheating
of someone you loved
so profoundly
and trusted completely,
because you misread
the intention in their heart.

Scream blood-curdling out loud
to release your anger
or quietly weep
to soothe your sorrow.

Attend to your wounds.
Then take hold of your part
for all that went wrong
and commit to moving on.

Gut-Wrenching

Sensitivity and empathy
do not make me a weakling.
I deserve to fully live in
and own the emotions I'm feeling.

I will wail loudly and wallow wildly
until my tears are dried of weeping,
as this unbearable pain
has crucial lessons to teach me.

Only then can I fully claim
that my heart has begun healing.

Crucial Lessons

You can have all the support
in the world until it's not.
You will feel their love flowing
like gold until it abruptly stops.
Just know that they were
with you for the wrong reason.
It is best you know now
that they were never your people.

Some relationships last a season;
others are eternally essential.
Despite the regard you held
for them, it was not mutual.
Note your lessons and run wild
into your unbridled future.

Seasoned People

Those who are wired like us,

fight to create our peace,

day after day, rebuilding trust,

keeping ourselves together

through the unbending months.

Perpetual survivors, we torch

the dark we dare to confront.

Perpetual

Word had come in the morning
that he was gone.
My battered heart lay
motionless and cold.
I felt nothing.

Neither sorrow
nor forgiveness
dared to bare witness
to all the suffering
he had wrought.

Death did not dissolve
or reinstate
my lost years to pain,
did little to release me
from the paralyzing shame.

Though I will not sing
sad gospel hymnals,
I grieve for a happy life...
the one I could have
been living all along.

Numbed

I am at deep peace in this moment,
feeling an unexpected reverence
for the formidable woman
I have become.
Restoring myself was hard won.

Restoring

A mountain, towering tall and proud,
I am immovable, never bowing down.
Though my enemies rage, petulant and loud,
I remain firm, unyielding, and headstrong.

Pain and adversity may appear and go.
My joy and trauma will lift and fall
as storms rail against me once more.
Never shaken, I am built to survive it all.

A Mountain

It has taken her years to build
herself into an austere glacier
that shipwrecks adversity
and freezes out the haters,
saving her from the certainty
of buckling beneath the weight
of her slow-moving dominion.

She proudly wears her crown
and, with one piercing glance,
will summarily ice you down.

Ice Princess

The fear of truly living
bled through my skin
despite my valiant efforts
to keep my dread hidden.

I stained every relationship
with the gray self-disdain
that I bathed myself in,
believing my own lies.

I could not trust anyone
to hear the silent cries
that I dared to hold in,
hide from the unforgiving.

Though I continue to struggle
to sustain my courage,
I have made improving me
my new top priority.

Silent Cries

In the end, your standards
outgrew his capacity to reach,
set new levels or grow.
His obliviousness outpaced
your willingness to teach
so, it is time to let go.

Mismatched

Not everyone abuses their welcome,
but some are predisposed
to believe you owe them
and will overuse their privilege.

Your loyalty should be earned,
never required or demanded.
Step back and unlearn
being taken for granted.

Hold onto your devotion
and unyielding service
until they put in the effort
to truly deserve it.

Unlearning

Learning to love and accept

her body as an imperfect vessel,

a home that reflects and honors

her beautiful spirit,

was the most uplifting lesson

she had ever been gifted.

Imperfect Vessel

That trembling girl whose
innocence was stolen
has grown into a strong
and magnificent woman
who uses her truth
as an illuminating light,
amplifying her voice
to lend support and strength,
especially to those alone
in a similar plight.

Illuminated

I will never settle

for merely existing

as your protected secret.

I am far worthier

than you treat me

and more enlightened

than you have perceived.

No Secret

Emotionally tattered, repeatedly battered,
she gallantly rallied her courage.
She elevated her well-being, rescued herself,
and safely secured both her mind and body.

For years she endured paralyzing pain,
a barrage of insults, and targeted wrongs.
Yet her swell of pride and high honor,
that valiant spirit, kept her lifted and strong.

Undaunted Spirit

Respect your fear, but stand strong,
even if you must go it alone.
A life of adverse experiences
has built you into an enduring spirit.
Embrace your next phase
and get on with living it.

Enduring

If you have never known
your biological father or mother,
grew up feeling alone,
or was made to feel othered
because your parents' lives
took an alternate path
that did not include you,
know that your life was no mistake.

Whether conceived in love
or an act of haste or hate,
upon taking that first life
sustaining breath,
you have never been forsaken.
This is your truth.
No need to wait for someone
else to exclaim it.
Celebrate the wonder
of your existence.

You are a delightful gift
to this miraculous world,
a rare collection of stardust
from on high, lightyears above.
It is time to re-gift yourself
and reclaim intrinsic love.
Lift up your wise eyes,
and let your shiny person particles
come alive in the starlight.
You are a treasured prize.

Treasured Prize

End the self-punishing.
Every fault you have
dutifully claimed
has been long forgiven.

Rejoice in the splendor
that ignites you within.
Own the life story
you have been given.

Your Splendor

My mind is an insulating vault
that keeps me sane,
locking away the trauma
this worn body has sustained.

Molten rivulets of steel
power through these robust veins,
forming me into a fortress
against the ravages life brings.

I remain secure and unwavering
against every strike of tormenting pain.

My Vault

Long after the vile acts end,
the impact of abuse continues.
Despite our many attempts,
we cannot smother or outlive
the recurrent nightmare.

It stalks the walls of our veins
spreading like an infection,
an uninhibited mutating of DNA,
injecting our somatic memory
with paralysis, so our muscles
never forget the sin.

We fight like combatants
to reject the disgust and shame
that collude to claim us.
Despite it all,
we refuse to fall victim
to generational disdain.

Muscle Memory

Some may consider
you aloof and artic cold,
due to the height of the standards
you choose to uphold.
Their perspective
does not belong in your story.
Protect your principles.
Keep reaching for glory.

Principles

Some days you bounce out of bed to do whatever it takes to drive yourself forward, conjure the courage out of nowhere to get going and complete that challenge.

Then there are days when you grant yourself grace, as you understand that no matter how hard you steel your face or press onward, you are just not up to your best performance.

Despite your talent, you will not be transforming into a superheroine today and that is okay. Knowing your strengths, weaknesses, triggers, and priorities allows you to strike a managing balance.

You don't need to win every daily sprint. Pause and reflect on your accomplishments over the years and the past few months. Stop punishing yourself for being imperfect and celebrate your abundant progress.

Grant Grace

There was no word you didn't say,
emotion left unconveyed
nor a thing did or failed to do,
just a building eventuality
that neither of us could accept.

A punctuated certain end
has become our reality,
despite how well we both
sidestepped our challenges.

Punctuated

Then there was nothing left.
Yet, she forgave herself
for saving someone else,
having put them first,
and amplifying their worth
to her own detriment.

She learned, grew, and healed.

Now she celebrates her every
accomplishment
along with those
of family and friends.
She marvels at this new
balanced version of herself.

Balanced Growth

I can sit and cower in the dark
or kick the doors wide open.
I can shield my breakable heart
or let it roam free and vulnerable.

I can allow fear to break me apart
or hold myself together.
I choose to make a bold new start
racing through life untethered.

Bold New Start

Your goal may feel impossible
until you have reached it.
Stone walls are an obstacle
before you breach them.

The fated fight will feel lost
until you have irrefutably won.
Hold fiercely and confidently
to the power of action you own.

Let your fire burn raging hot,
then simmer it on low.
Just never let your heart's
desires or dreams go.

You are poised to erupt
into a wild blaze of flames
with just the right setting
and a steady flow of oxygen.

Go light the world up
and put your fears to shame.
You are ready to own
whatever life brings!

Breach Walls

No matter how difficult the tests,

I will never permit life's regrets

to steal away my blessedness.

Intended Blessings

You deserve to shamelessly shed
uninhibited happy tears,
yielded from the sacrifices
you sowed for years
in the stoic silence.

Leap high and scream loud.
Yes, deliriously shout
your delight and elation.
Offer no one an apology
for celebrating you
or your dream life come true.

Happy Tears

I cannot find the perfect ones,
those words that will right everything,
nor help you understand my why.

I decided that this moment is my now.
It is simply time I reclaim my reality
and release the fantasy that was us.

My Moment

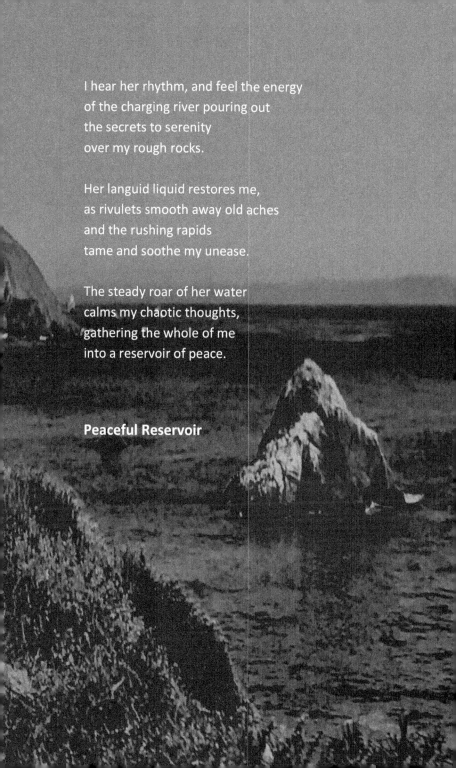

I hear her rhythm, and feel the energy
of the charging river pouring out
the secrets to serenity
over my rough rocks.

Her languid liquid restores me,
as rivulets smooth away old aches
and the rushing rapids
tame and soothe my unease.

The steady roar of her water
calms my chaotic thoughts,
gathering the whole of me
into a reservoir of peace.

Peaceful Reservoir

Though she cannot outrun
life's poisons or injuries,
nor undo the harm
of the threatening memory
that slowly unravels
the protective blanket
swaddling her soul,
she works diligently every day
rising above her burdens
to remain connected
and fully whole.

Remain Whole

She embraces the culpability
for the life choices she's made,
especially those that have
caused her personal delays,
stunted her success,
and dulled her happiness.

She is reversing this ill-fated run
and turning this train around.
The past cannot be undone,
but she is making new decisions
that will soon overshadow
her archaic fails and blunders.

Culpable

There are a few things in life
you cannot bounce back from;
a shattered heart and a rough start
are high on the list among them.

Get on with living the life
you have been seeking.
The universe did not create you
to tremble like a timid weakling.

On with Living

Today ends the weeping.
I have willed salty tears away
and assessed the damage.
No longer the vulnerable prey,
I am stripping off old bandages
to expose my scars to the light of day.

I am wiser than yesterday,
far stronger than the challenges
tomorrow will send my way.
I have grown newfound courage
and am assured I will be okay.

End of Weeping

Leaving my pain unhealed
revealed a truth I could not see__
that I was undermining
the person I was born to be.

Being strong does not mean
I should ignore the wrong,
it is facing anything
that threatens to harm me head-on.

Head On

You no longer command
my rapt attention,
conjure warm emotions
or ignite bile anguish.

I feel neither love nor hate
when I hear your name.
Seeing you or not
is just the same.

You only exist between
the never should haves
and the hard lessons learned
on the list of things
I did that were dumb.

Indifference is the place
I go when the healing is done.
I am in the right headspace,
as all you evoke is numb.

Indifference

There is nothing better
lurking on the other
side of never.

Place yourself in the spaces
that encourage your mind
to imagine and embrace
your best life.

Fight for your inspired vision
with all your might.

Nothing Better

Self-healing is deepening

the love residing in me,

strengthening the gravity

that is anchoring me

and broadening my possibilities.

Finally, fixing old maladies

fills my life with new meaning.

New Meaning

Sustaining a positive mental place
and healthy wellbeing
can seem precarious.

Existing in a happy state
is a wild swinging pendulum,
a thrilling fluid existence
fueled by rich moments
that are so kinetic
they can spiral out of control
before I can catch hold.

This life journey is fragile,
but I refuse to miss
its joy rides for anything.

Kinetic Moments

I am detaching my feelings
from people who refuse
to acknowledge,
or see the whole of me.

All my wasted energy
will be redirected
and channeled
into lifting my deflated spirits.

Detach

You are no longer that same you.
No, not the one who believed
the best answers were the ones you knew.
Too naïve to dance around questions,
so eager to start life's journey,
that you torched the earth
you were standing upon
before your secret dreams
could grow roots and take hold.

Burned too often, you retreated
to care for your wounds.
You forged a new path
and set a rhythm for living
where true connections
would be nurtured to last,
even when you could not name
exactly what you were after.

Throughout your discovery journey,
you filled souls with laughter
and broadened smiles on faces
in the remotest of places.
You stumbled. You failed.
Yet, in life, you always excelled.
Through it all, your aura grew.
The essence of you filtered through.
Though often uncomfortable,
you reveled with pleasure
at evolving into your strongest version.

Your Aura

Struggle stripped away
my non-essential.
Being knocked to my knees,
then stumbling
back to where I started
was humbling.
The work to recover
gave me clarity,
chiseling me into
a hardened survivor.

Survivor

Defeated, but I am not broken.
This test is far from over.
I brush those old failures
off my heavy shoulders,
and reject the very notion.

I will run warp speed
until my wings lift high
and spread fully open.

Uplifted by the wind,
soon I will be flying
high above life's oceans,
eclipsing the horizon,
setting new dreams in motion.

I dare not give up, nor in.
I will never let go.
I came to life to win.

Eclipse the Horizon

You are the provider
> who dared to give.

Your strength runs deeper
> than your pain.

You are the survivor
> who fought to live,

Yes, the triumphant one
> who at last overcame.

Triumphant

Even after all they have done
to destroy your will to fight,
and attempt to shut you down,
your compassion and light
continues to burn,
still outshines their might,
completely overshadowing them.

Keep your face to the sun.
Your flame is eternally lit
by the spiritual energy
emanating from deep within.

Face the Sun

Healing Grace

Hold firmly to your glory.
Write a new ending,
ripe with rich wisdom
from the worn pages
of your traumatic,
yet inspiring story.

New Ending

You are the face I see
when I tell my most
extraordinary love story.
Hello Me.

Falling in love with myself
without conditions,
accepting my talents and flaws
and owning my poor decisions
are my proudest life victories.

My Greatest Love

When the tides of life
rise high and roar to my shore,
my courage remains resolute.

As I dismantle each fear
my confidence soars,
uplifted by my principles.

Holding the power over
the direction of my life
makes me feel invincible.

Resolute

You are resilient enough

to fight your way through it,

and annihilate anything

trying to keep you from living.

Unleash the fierce lioness

that rules your spirit.

Lioness

It has taken a lifetime
of lost journeys,
a body riddled with painful
knocks and bruises,
years of broken promises,
honest mistakes
and months of wrong turns
to finally learn
that I am an outstanding
and worthy human.

Worthy Human

I am a rugged boulder,
pushing back the storm
that attempts to move
and manipulate me.

I withstand intense shocks
sent to shake me,
fending off anything
and anyone who dares to break me.

Unmovable

Healing Grace

I am pressing onward
through this fire.
Emboldened, I rise
from the hot ashes
fueled by raw ire.
Though fear flames
farther than I can see,
my phoenix wings lift
and finally spring me free.
Though I may be burned,
not even fate can break me.

From the Ashes

Though my body is weary,
my fragile ego wounded,
and my heart lay wedged open,
I will retrace my mistakes,
collect and dispatch them
all to the distant past.

I will never abandon me.
Therefore, I will forgive myself
of present transgressions
and future missteps.
I clothed my soul in grace
for every breath I take.

Healing Grace

*Whatever you
are going through,
allow yourself
measured time
and
Healing Grace.
Continue to climb.
You were meant
to soar!*

OTHER BOOKS

by Michelle G. Stradford

Inspirational Poetry

I'm Rising: Determined. Confident. Powerful.

Rise Unstoppable

Self Love Notes II: Affirming Poetry & Prose

Self Love Notes: Uplifting Poetry, Affirmations & Quotes

Romantic Love Poetry

Waves of You: Love Poems

When Love Rises

I'm Rising: Determined. Confident. Powerful

Rise Unstoppable

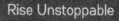

I was broken
and tired of hiding,
when finally
I held up the mirror
to peer at my fractured parts,
and saw that
pain and struggle
had not twisted me
into something angry,
unrecognizable and hideous,
but into a courageous,
bolder, and more
formidable me.

Formidable

She tugged firmly
on a thin thread of faith
untied herself, just let go,
and released her fear of
unraveling.

She watched herself unspool,
her magic unfolding
into infinite potential.

Unravel

SCAN QR CODE TO GET A SIGNED COPY OF BOOK

FROM THE AUTHOR

I am grateful you completed reading *"Healing Grace."* I hope you found comfort, affinity, and inspiration in the poetry and prose.

Feedback, whether a phrase, a brief sentence or a paragraph, is valued and appreciated. Your input helps me validate my themes and informs me about what I should write next. So, please take a moment to leave a rating and review online at the retailer site where you purchased this book.

To stay updated on my next book release, read samples of work in progress, etc., please connect with me:

TikTok @michellestradford
Instagram @michellestradfordauthor
Twitter @mgstradford
Facebook @michellestradfordauthor
Pinterest @michellestradfordauthor
Bookbub: michelle-g-stradford
Goodreads: Michelle G Stradford

 Subscribe to my newsletter for book release updates, promotions, and giveaways by scanning code or search https://linktr.ee/michellestradford

...ve Notes: Uplifting Poetry, ...ffirmations & Quotes

Self Love Notes II: Affirm... Poetry & Prose

Someday I will grow
brave enough
...o carefully unfurl my secrets
and watch them free-fall
in velvet blankets,
like the petals of a rose
finally discovering
the beauty of freedom
now that they
are no longer trapped
inside the folds
of my soul.

My Secrets

You are far stronger
than you have imagined.
Never underestimate
your capacity to battle
your fiercest enemy
then soar high
despite the damage
sustained by your wings.

Soar Steadily

ACKNOWLEDGMENTS

I offer my heartfelt thanks to my husband and daughters for their love and support. They breathe life into everything I do.

I extend my sincere thank you to the readers who continue to purchase and read my books. Those of you who share how my words have encouraged you or helped others keep me going. I am grateful to each of you.

EXCERPTS FROM ROMANTIC COLLECTION

Waves of You: Love Poems

When Love Rises

Your love does not
take my breath away.
It breathes life into me,
no matter how high
you lift my soul
or how deep
you send me
searching.

I inhaled the breath
you exhaled
and in a singular moment
we breathed life
into this
extraordinary love.

Soul Search

Kissed to Life

SCAN QR CODE TO GET A SIGNED COPY OF BOOK

ABOUT THE AUTHOR

Michelle G. Stradford is a bestselling Author, Architect, Artist, and Photographer who creates written, visual, and inhabitable art. Her writing style is contemporary free-verse, as her goal is to create poetry and prose that is relatable and inspiring to her readers. Besides poetry, she has authored short stories and fiction since adolescence.

Michelle strives to use her experiences and writing to build a platform encouraging women and girls to own their power, overcome challenges and attain their goals. She is married and has two daughters.

Printed in Great Britain
by Amazon